CW00428563

A Little Oasis

THE EARLY HISTORY OF ASHTON PARK

WEST KIRBY

by

Barbara Mason

This book is dedicated to the memory of my grandfather,
Edward Hadwin,
the second park-keeper and to the friends of Ashton Park who have
worked so hard to make improvements there in recent years.

Barbara Mason

First published 1996 by Countyvise Limited, 1 & 3 Grove Road, Rock Ferry, Birkenhead, Wirral, Merseyside L42 3XS in conjunction with the author Barbara Mason.

Copyright © 1996 Barbara Mason

. The right of Barbara Mason to be identified as the author of this work has been asserted by her in accordance with the Copyright, Designs and Patents Act 1988.

British Library Cataloguing in Publication Data.
A catalogue record for this book is available from the British Library.

ISBN 0 907768 97 0

All rights reserved. No part of this publication may be reproduced, stored in a retrieval system, or transmitted, in any form, or by any means, electronic, chemical, mechanical, photocopying, recording or otherwise, without the prior permission of the publisher.

i

Contents

List of Illustrations

Acknowledgements

In compiling this booklet I owe a debt of gratitude to:-

Mrs. Lucy Smith and her son James on recollections of Joseph James Stanley, the first Park-keeper;

Mrs. Dolly Shipman who worked as a gardener in the Park during the First World War;

Mary Ward, Tutor, and my colleagues on the Diploma in Local History Course at Wirral Metropolitan College, Birkenhead;

Dave Thompson, Archivist, and Carol Bidston, Local History Archivist, Wirral Borough Council, Central Library, Birkenhead, and helpful staff;

Charles Connor, Secretary, of 'Friends of Ashton Park' for sharing information and documents;

Tom Wayles of 'Tom Gardener' who helped identify trees and shrubs in the Park;

Relations and friends who generously supplied photos;

and last but not least

My husband Geoff who has 'lived' with the Ashton Park project for the past year and for his encouragement.

Introduction

By the beginning of this century almost every town of any size had its parks and gardens. These were a source of pride to Local Authorities alongside other public works and utilities.

Ashton Park, West Kirby, developed from the natural desire of the District Council to create a little oasis where residents and visitors could enjoy simple pleasures and pastimes in a healthy and sheltered environment.

My interest in the Park sprang mainly from the proposed Centenary Celebrations and a close family connection - my Grandfather, Edward Hadwin, was the second Park-keeper to be appointed. There was also a lack of published material on this popular amenity.

There were many difficulties and delays in establishing Ashton Park and a study of the local Parks and Gardens Committee minutes, newspaper accounts and other sources have revealed these. In this booklet, with the aid of personal recollections and memorabilia, it is hoped to present a picture for you of the Park in its early years.

BARBARA MASON

Chapter One

Development of West Kirby

Can you imagine what West Kirby was like near the end of the last century?

A description in the Hoylake and West Kirby Directory of 1897 pointed to its future as a residential health resort, stressing:-

> "... varied and beautiful series of land and seascapes. Its climate may be said to be almost as varied as its scenery. ... West Kirby has a mean temperature as high and as even as any watering place in the South of England and is becoming famed for its beneficial effects in consumption and other diseases of the respiratory organs... " [1]

West Kirby was contrasted with its sister township of Hoylake, which was becoming equally famous for its strong, pure and bracing influences.

The district had begun to develop with the advent of the railway and building of good roads. In 1871 Hoylake and West Kirby had a population of only 2,100 and by 1891 this had risen to 6,545. With the growth in population a more efficient form of local government was needed. Local boards were formed, which led eventually to an Urban District Council and, although West Kirby applied to become a separate entity, this was refused and in 1897 Hoylake took precedence. The bulk of the population was living in Hoylake at that time and the Town Hall was built there in the same year.

The Council made great strides in the next decade. Promenades were built in both townships with a Marine Lake at West Kirby. An Electric Lighting Station opened in 1901, Public Halls were erected and water and sewerage systems were installed. New houses were built and shops opened to accommodate the expanding community.

Chapter Two

Difficulties and Delays

By the end of the 19th Century public parks were a normal inclusion in any Urban District or small town's development.

Ashton Park was first mentioned in the minutes of Hoylake and West Kirby Urban District Council in 1896. It was laid out over several years on land called Cow Hey, which was owned by Miss Ashton of London, also on a section of Glebe land along the adjoining Church side, which was part of the income of St. Bridget's Church. Both these sections of land were at first leased to the Council.

In June, 1898, Miss Ashton's solicitors wrote to the Council complaining of the delay in taking up the land from their client. Draft leases went to and fro to the Council and were duly amended. Miss Ashton's Solicitors finally negotiated a yearly rent of £156. 16s. 7d. (£156.83p) in 1899 and Canon Blencowe, the Rector of St. Bridget's Church, agreed a rent of £46 per annum.

Everything had to be negotiated through Solicitors, one example being the footbridge over the London and North Western and Great Western Joint Railway. This railway divided the Park into two and ran from West Kirby to Parkgate, opening in 1885. The bridge cost £257. 10s. (£257.50p) and was built by Messrs. Bruce and Still of Liverpool. Portions of land for entrances to the Park were transferred or rejected by the Council. Railings along Carpenter's Lane had to be sanctioned by Miss Ashton's agents and the laying out of the Park was postponed until October, 1899. In May 1900 there were complaints from Mrs. A. Larkin of West Kirby re trespass on land by carts engaged on laying out of the Park. (There

3

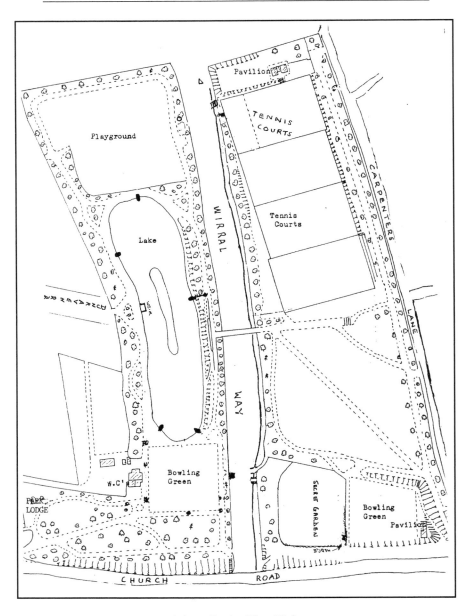

Ashton Park - West Kirby

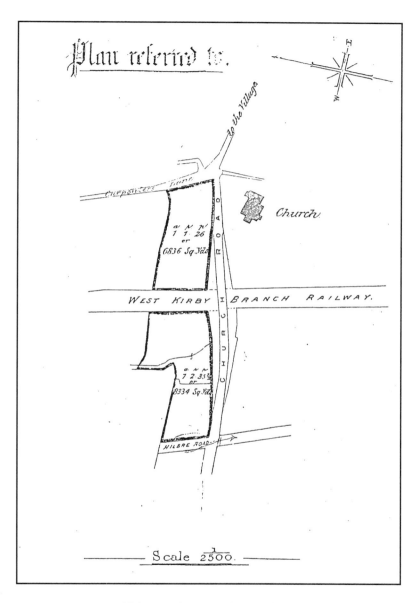

Glebe Land - St. Bridget's Church

5

were three Larkin brothers who farmed land in Rectory Road).

The Council had trouble with the firm who supplied the railings who did not want to complete the contract at the original price which had been quoted a year previously. A further complaint was made a few months later and, failing delivery, the Surveyor was authorised to purchase elsewhere at the expense of the contractor. In 1901 a draft contract was approved with Messrs. Brown and Backhouse for the erection of the Park Lodge and lavatories at West Kirby Park at a cost of £470 and £75 respectively. The Lower and Upper parks were laid out at separate times. In 1900 a tender for supply and planting of trees was accepted from Messrs. Dickson's Ltd., Chester, at a cost of £65. 19s.0d. (£65. 95p).

Joseph James Stanley, The First Park-Keeper
1901 - 1911

Chapter Three

Appointment of the first Park-Keeper

In December 1900 the Parks Committee agreed that:-

'a gardener be engaged for West Kirby Park at a wage of 25/- (£1.25p) per week, the appointment to be reconsidered when the lodge is created'. [2]

Twenty applications were received and the Chairman (Mr. Bell) with Mr. Smith, a Councillor, were requested to draw up a short list. On the 16th January, 1901, Mr. J.J. Stanley of West Kirby was appointed as Gardener, in accordance with the terms of the advertisement.

Joseph James Stanley was born in January, 1871, and came to Ashton Park at the relatively early age of 30.

Mr. Stanley worked first as a gardener in private service for a Mrs. Falk (later Lady Rachael Falk) who lived in a house in Wetstone Lane.

The Lodge was still being built so it was not until July, 1901 that Mr. Stanley was granted the tenancy. He moved there with his wife and two young daughters. Two boys were later born at the house. The Council agreed to pay rates and taxes in addition to his wage of 25/- per week as Park-keeper.

In an interview with Mrs. Lucy Smith who was Mr. Stanley's second daughter and a baby of one year old when they moved to the Park Lodge, she recalled her early days there. It had, she says, no electricity then. There were oil lamps downstairs and candles were used upstairs. There was no wallpaper on the walls because it was newly plastered. There was a bathroom (1907 when a hot water system was installed) but no indoor toilet.

The Park Lodge from an original drawing by Wil McManus

10ᵗʰ MARCH 1900

Local Government Board Inquiry.

On Wednesday last, Mr. H. Percy Boulnois, M. Inst. C.E., an inspector of the Local Government Board, held an inquiry into an application of the District Council for powers to borrow £2400, for the purpose of purchasing, laying out, and otherwise completing the new park at the Cowhey, West Kirby.

The law clerk (Mr. Roderick Williams) laid the main features of the scheme before the Inspector. He referred to the fact that most of the surrounding land was being built over, and showed that for the sake of the health, as well as the recreation of the inhabitants of the West Kirby part of the district, the proposed park would be a great advantage. He also said that the district was one much recommended by the medical faculty, and the park from its sheltered position would become an additional attraction, as a place where convalescents could enjoy the fresh air free from the dangers of injurious winds.

The surveyor (Mr. Foster) explained the plans of the proposed park with the lake, fences, gates, lodge, band stand, &c. He also showed the designs for a bridge over the railway from Darmonds green.

Mr. J. F. Ellison said he had resided in West Kirby for 16 years, had been a member of the District Council from its inception, and was well acquainted with the district and its needs. He believed the proposed park was required for the accommodation of visitors, and the scheme was one that had been advocated by the ratepayers for a long time, believing that such a place was needed to further the progress and general interests of the district.

Messrs. Bird and Smith intimated that the scheme had the approval of the District Council.

The Inspector afterwards visited the site of the proposed park, accompanied by Messrs. Ellison, Williams and Foster.

Newspaper Report from
"Herald and Visitor"
re: Local Government Board Inquiry 1900

In the meantime, work was going ahead on the laying out of the lower park. The Surveyor, Thomas Foster, had submitted an amended estimate, which included fencing for the next section and the footbridge over the railway, amounting to £2,400. This was accepted and the Council agreed to apply to the Local Government Board to borrow that amount over 30 years.

The newly appointed Park-Keeper requested some gardening tools and W. Ingham and D.H. Allan of Hoylake supplied lawn mowers. A few years later it was resolved that a donkey be acquired for mowing purposes in the Park. Mr. Stanley was also authorised to purchase plants amounting to £9. 14s. 2d. (£9.71p).

Bye-laws for the district were adopted by the Council in January, 1900, as follows:-

'for the prevention of nuisances arising from snow, filth, dust, ashes and rubbish' and for the 'prevention of keeping animals on premises so as to be injurious to health'. [3]

The Hoylake and West Kirby Herald and Visitor Newspaper commented that 'by the former of these we shall have to sweep in front of our own doorways, and the latter is aimed at such nuisances as piggeries and dog kennels kept so as to become a nuisance'. [4]

At one time the deposit of night soil refuse in the Park must have been allowed, or not objected to, because in July, 1901, the further deposit of such refuse was prohibited.

An evening inspection of the Park was made the same month, after which it was agreed that the position of the entrance gates in Hilbre Road be altered and the Surveyor was authorised to order the wire guard for the footbridge over the railway.

In October estimates were obtained for laying out of the Upper Park at a cost of £1,335. 19s. 0d. (£1,335.95p) with an additional £550 for seats, fencing, bridge slope and extra work in connection with the Band Stand terrace. A band stand and fountain, which had been proposed for the lower park, was not proceeded with. A water fountain was subsequently donated from Wilton Grange, Meols Drive, in 1913.

Twelve seats were ordered from Mr. William Hazlehurst of Hoylake but it was decided later not to purchase further seats and to put the money towards a propagating house which cost £36.

In July 1901 members of the Council were asking when the park was going to be opened to the public. The answer was that it would be another month as the walks had not been gravelled and that one of the main reasons for delay was the obstruction by the railway company. The Chairman wryly remarked that 'if they were going to wait for everything to be finished they would be a long time'. A month later a Councillor asked if the Park was now ready to be opened. The Chairman said it was practically completed and the Surveyor added that it would be another fortnight or three weeks at the outside. The expenditure on the making of West Kirby Park was queried. It was reported that the estimated cost had been £2,400 but £3,150 spent. A bandstand at a cost of £90 had still to be erected, plus a drinking fountain (£15) and two shelters (£70). The estimated excess in

The Old-Established Shop.

WILLIAM INGHAM,

FURNISHING IRONMONGER,

Cycle and China Dealer,

26, MARKET STREET,

HOYLAKE.

CYCLE ACCESSORIES AND REPAIRS.

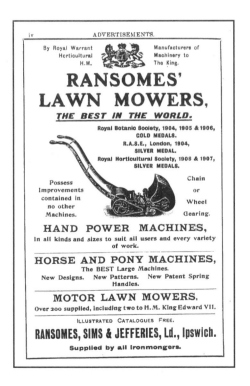

iv   ADVERTISEMENTS.

By Royal Warrant   Manufacturers of
Horticultural   Machinery to
H.M.   The King.

RANSOMES' LAWN MOWERS,

THE BEST IN THE WORLD.

Royal Botanic Society, 1904, 1905 & 1906,
GOLD MEDALS.
R.A.S.E., London, 1904,
SILVER MEDAL.
Royal Horticultural Society, 1906 & 1907,
SILVER MEDALS.

Possess   Chain
Improvements   or
contained in   Wheel
no other
Machines.   Gearing.

HAND POWER MACHINES,

In all kinds and sizes to suit all users and every variety
of work.

HORSE AND PONY MACHINES,

The BEST Large Machines.
New Designs.   New Patterns.   New Patent Spring
Handles.

MOTOR LAWN MOWERS,

Over 200 supplied, including two to H.M. King Edward VII.

ILLUSTRATED CATALOGUES FREE.

RANSOMES, SIMS & JEFFERIES, Ld., Ipswich.

Supplied by all Ironmongers.

Mrs J.W. Glover (neé Summerfield) and Family (1903)

The Park Lodge by Night

expenditure would be £925, only 2d. in the £1 on the rates. A Mr. Ellison said the footbridge had cost a good deal more on account of demands by the Railway Company for sinking of the foundation to greater depths than had been anticipated. The Lodge had also cost £470 due to a rise in the price of building material. The original estimate had been £300. The Surveyor remarked that the estimates had been made five or six years ago and that the excavation of the lake had caused delays too. The cost of building the Lodge itself was controversial as the following comments in the Birkenhead News for September 7th, 1901, reveal:-

> "To a commodious dog kennel I have heard likened the house which has been erected at a cost, I believe, of about £400 for the keeper of West Kirby Park. A prominent Hoylake gentleman with whom I conversed on the subject said that if he could not erect as good, or even better, a house for £150 he would eat his - well, an indispensable article of apparel worn in close proximity to his skin. At the same time I am told that the inhabitants of the house are satisfied with it, unpretentious though it may be. Nevertheless, while they are about, the committee might have built with some degree of ornamentation and in keeping with the architectural beauties of the neighbourhood." [5]

The Birkenhead News reporter wondered by August 24th whether the Park would ever be finished and on 14th September the following comments were made in that newspaper:-

> "Appropos of the West Kirby Park, although apparently it is now finished, no one seems to definitely know when it will be opened. Of a certain gentleman in authority inquiries as to the probable date of opening and other particulars were being made. Asked if he thought there would be any opening ceremony he said, 'No, I don't think it will run like that. I think they'll just open it and let the public in."[6]

This is what appears to have happened and, although the Lower Park had been completed, the Upper Park was still being laid out in October, 1901.

Lucy Smith recalls that there was a constant crush of people walking through the lower park, including many invalids in bath chairs, because West Kirby was a place for retired and elderly people coming on holiday. There were also children accompanied by nursemaids in uniform, bonnet and veil, which was another sign of Edwardian days. The people pushing the bath chairs were elderly men who, she thinks, were paid a fee of 8d.

an hour. The Park Lodge was some kind of social focus being relatively new. Visitors used to call and ask questions and sometimes they used to ask for a glass of water, so Mrs. Stanley, Lucy's mother, used to see quite a lot of visitors at the Park Lodge.

A slightly satirical letter appeared in the "Herald and Visitor" in September, 1901, showing that the park was used by the public by then:-

'Yesterday we took a little walk in the New Park, West Kirby. We marshalled the family and made a tour of inspection, up and down and round and round the cinder avenues and the cobble walks, between the grassy borders and the flower and shrub plantations. We mused awhile on the iron bridge at midday and fed imaginary swans on the imaginary lake in the imaginary future. This lake (a ducky little lakelet) is said to be quite 2 inches deep! Of course it is a little wider and longer. With the present rainy season and the aid of a few kind friends with watering cans, I think we might get it up to 3 inches, say, and keep that as concert pitch. We might be able, if sufficient space is left in the park, to accommodate any probable statues of local heroes or patrons, which we are almost sure to need as time goes on and the size of our local history book increases. A park is nothing without a monument or two.' [7]

Early photograph of Ashton Park

15

THE HERALD AND VISITOR—SATURDAY, JANUARY

THE YEAR'S RECORD, 1899.

We give below a record of the principal local events which have occurred during the year 1899 as recorded in the columns of the HERALD.

JANUARY.

2—Terrific Gale: Chimneys blown down and severe damage done throughout the district.
—The flat Sefton, of Liverpool, was wrecked on the shore near Leasowe Lighthouse.
3—Opening of New Wings to West Kirby Parish Schools by the very Rev. the Dean of Chester.
5—Another Terrific Storm: The spray on West Kirby Promenade rose to a height of over 50 feet. The Hoylake promenade was covered with water. The "Anglican" fishing boat was driven ashore near Shaw's "battery." No. 12 Red Buoy broke from her moorings. Much damage was also done to house property throughout the district.
9—Inauguration of Sanatorium for consumptives at West Kirby.
10—Farmers' and Tradesmens' Ball at West Kirby.
—Issue of Order of County Council re-constituting the Wirral Board of Guardians and giving eight instead of five guardians to the Urban District.
16—District Council Meeting: Appointment of Meola Commons Committee. Mr. Wannop's resignation accepted.
21—Resignation of Mr. C. Roberts from the District Council.
25—Break-down on the Railway between Hoylake and West Kirby, through several wagons being thrown off the line, serious delay in the traffic.
31—Nominations of Messrs. Walter Lowndes and H. Neville Bewley to the seat vacated by Mr. Wannop.
—Annual Meeting of Golf Club: Election of Mr. W. S. Patterson as captain.

FEBRUARY.

2—Volunteer Ball in Hoylake.
2—Death of Mr. James Parr, of Church road, Hoylake.
8—Grand Orchestral Concert: Visit of Mr. Wm. Ludwig.
16—Inauguration of the North Ward Ratepayers Association.
18—Election of Mr. W. Lowndes to the District Council by a majority of 111 over Mr. H. Neville Bewley.
20—Meeting of District Council:
27—Presentation of a bookcase and address to the Rev. J. C. Thomas, by the members of the Presbyterian Church, Hoylake.
28—Lecture on Westminster Abbey by Rev. Jas. H. Martyn.

MARCH.

1—Installation of Mr. W. H. Middleton-Andrews as W.M. of West Kirby Masonic Lodge.
3—Death of Mr. George Hazlehurst, smith and farrier, of Hoylake.
7—Biograph Entertainment at the Tynwald Hall.
8—Inaugural Meeting of the scheme for providing hospital wards in the Children's Convalescent Home; address by Dr. Wm. Carter.
9—Nominations for Election of District Councillors and Guardians.
11—Charity Match between Hoylake and Wirral Ramblers for the funds of the Nursing Institution.
—Final P.S.E. at the Tynwald Hall, the Mayor of Birkenhead presiding.
14—Enthusiastic Meeting on behalf of Mr. Tom Davies' candidature for the North Ward.
20—Meeting of District Council—the charges of Mr. Ezard against Mr. Richard Bird entirely disproved.
23—Presentation to Mrs. Kirkland by her Bible Class in connection with the Presbyterian Church, West Kirby.
25—District Council Election: Triumphant return of Messrs. T. Davies, R. Bird, J. F. Smith (North Ward), W. A. Jones (South Ward), and J. Royston (Central Ward).
—Guardian Election: The first lady guardian (Mrs. Dalglish) elected to represent this district. Messrs. Aldred and Townsend also elected in addition to Messrs. Gill, Christian, Lea, Richards and the Rev. F. Sanders.
29—Death of Mr. Hugh Hughes, of the Green Lodge Hotel.

APRIL.

2—Serious fire in Cable road.
5—Wreck of the flat "Tryfan" on Leasowe shore.
7—Death of Mr. Arthur Anderson of Hoylake.
10—Annual display at West Kirby Gymnasium.
—District Council Meeting: Business mostly "valedictory."
12—Marriage of Miss Margaret Ellison to Mr. John Edward Green.
13—Hoylake Lifeboat assist. a flat in danger on the North Bank.
17—Annual Meeting of District Council.
24—Special Meeting of District Council to protest against the making of a goods station near Kirby Park by the Joint Railways.
25—Baptism of "Joan Hildeburgh," infant daughter of Mr. John Glynn—the first baptism in St. Hildeburgh's Church.
27—Opening of Spring Meeting of Royal Liverpool Golf Club.
28—Formation of the local branch of the Pentecostal League.
28—Body of man picked up on the shore at Hoylake—being that of a man named John Owen, one of the crew of Hopper No. 5, sunk in the Mersey on the same day.
30—Inauguration of regular Sunday evening services at the Meols Schoolroom.

MAY.

1—Opening of St. Hildeburgh's Church: First sermon preached by the Ven. Archdeacon Barber.
—Formation of the Hoylake and West Kirby Tradesmen's Protection Society.
3—Local Government Board Inquiry on proposals to borrow £818 for improving and widening Market street and also £865 for purchasing horses and wagons.
6—Permanent enlargement of the HERALD AND VISITOR to eight pages.
—Death of Mr. Woolley, of the Parade, Hoylake.
12—Sudden death of a boy at Meols Camp.
15—Commencement of the Stage Coach "Comet" running through this district from Chester.
—District Council Meeting; Protest of Ratepayers against the Council's action. Demand for Petty Sessions Court supported by resolution.
18—Mr. George Wise lectures at West Kirby on the "Crisis in the Church."
23—Burglary at Mr. Brewer's jewellers shop, West Kirby.
24—Queen's Birthday: Royal Salute on shore at Hoylake by the 67th Battery Royal Artillery.
29—Mr. John Ball, jun., won the Amateur Golf Championship for the fifth time.
31—Conviction and severe sentence on boys for placing upright nails on the roadway at Meols so as to puncture cycle tyres.
—Disorderly meeting at West Kirby in connection with tip-wagon agitation.

JUNE.

2—Annual Meeting of Hoylake Conservative Association.
3—Caldy Grange Grammar School Annual Sports.
3—Grand Jerusalem Bazaar at Christian Institute.
—Formation of the Hoylake Homing Society.
3—Harry Vardon wins the Open Golf Championship at Sandwich with an aggregate score of 310 for four rounds.
10—Trip to Burton by employees of Messrs. Mills, of West Kirby and Liscard.
16—Presentation by the Royal National Lifeboat Institution of a reward for life saving to Captain Samuel Armitage and a boat's crew.
19—District Council Meeting.
21—Picnic of the B.W.T.A. to Storeton.

28—Heavy Thunderstorm over the District.
—Banquet to Mr. John Ball, junr., at Leasowe Club.

JULY.

1—Hilbre Lifeboat rescue a yacht off West Hoyle.
5—Grange Club Annual Dinner.
8—Death of Mr. George Miller, of Hoylake.
9—Flower Service at the Parish Church, Hoylake.
12—Marriage of Miss Salvidge to Captain Breech at West Kirby Church.
15—Mr. Chrimes' Workpeople's Trip to Llangollen.
17—Meeting of the District Council.
19—Marriage of Dr. Bicknell to Miss Ada Mack, and sad death of the bride's mother on the following day.
20—Death of Mr. William Croxton, aged 88.
22—Trip of Workpeople to Blackpool: Employees of Messrs. W. C. White, George Booth, W. Burkey, and W. Hughes.
— Vicar's Bible Class Excursion to Bettws-y-Coed.
24—Death of Mr. James Eccles, aged 83 years.
26—Visit of Clatterbridge Workhouse Inmates to West Kirby.
29—Hoylake Regatta.

AUGUST.

6—Lifeboat Sunday—Sermon in Hoylake Parish Church by the Rev. A. Hamilton King.
7—Accident to Chief Coastguardsman Hicks while at the Naval Manoeuvres at the Isle of Man.
12—Excursion of Mr. W. W. Christian's employees to Blackpool.
14—Opening of New Pavillion at West Kirby Bowling Green by Mr. W. H. Middleton-Andrews.
17—Fourth Annual Cycle Carnival and Lantern Parade.
19—Final of Village Play Golf Tournament.
21—District Council Meeting: Stormy protest on the subject of the Wirral Railway Service.
24—Great gorse fire on Grange Hill.
26—Supplementary Regatta to run off extra races and sports.
27—Break down of a pumping engine at the Water Works, and stoppage of supply of water for several hours on Sunday morning.
30—Primrose League Pic-nic to Caergwrle Castle.

SEPTEMBER.

1—John Ball jun., wins the Irish Golf Championship by 3 up and 2 to play.
2—Drowning of Mr. Norman Lange and Mr. Frame by the capsizing of a boat at Beaumaris.
5—Shocking death of Coastguardsman Lilley, of Hoylake, while assisting to launch the Hilbre Lifeboat.
—Opening of the Hoylake Working Men's Reading Room.
9—Funeral of Coastguardsman Lilley with full naval honours.
1—Presentation to Sergeant Eaton.
2—Cycle Carnival Concert and distribution of prizes.
13—Technical Instruction Classes—Distribution of Prizes.
17—Great Gales along the Coast with very high tides—continuing during the week.
18—District Council Meeting: Debate on the purchase of horses—lively time.
19—Finding of a porpoise on the lifeboat slip by Mr. Joseph Silcox.
22—Consecration of St. Hildeburgh's Church, by Dr. Jayne, Lord Bishop of Chester.
23—Meeting of Fishermen—nominations for the Fisheries Board.

OCTOBER.

1—Harvest Festival at several of the Churches.
2—Removal of Hoylake Post Office to new premises in Market street.
8—Visit of the Bishop of Shrewsbury to the Roman Catholic Church at West Kirby.
14—Death of Mr. Stanton Eddowes.
16—District Council Meeting: Debate on proposal to re-assess the district.
17—Local Government Inquiry: into borrowing money for Carpenters Lane sewer and lighting the Hoylake sewer buoys.
18—Early Closing Movement commenced—Wednesday at 4 p.m.
21—Opening Ceremony of West Kirby Marine Lake, with banquet in the evening.
—Funeral of Police-Sergeant Currie.
23—Special Meeting of District Council to consider and adopt new Parliamentary Bill.
30—Adjourned Special Meeting of the District Council to consider Parliamentary Bill.
31—Death of Mr. Harry Barber.

NOVEMBER.

4—Institution of the HERALD Transvaal War Fund.
—Opening of the Hospital Wards at the Children's Convalescent Home.
8—Annual Rehearsal of the Institute School, West Kirby.
10—Rescue of the schooner "Teaser" by the Hilbre Lifeboat.
—Lecture by Max O'Rell at West Kirby Literary Society.
11—Opening of the new Lifeboat House by Mrs Harold Wrigley.
13—Opening of new Public Hall, West Kirby, with a Grand Concert.
20—District Council Meeting.
23—Installation of Mr. John Morris as W.M. of the Hilbre Lodge.
25—Patriotic Concert at the new Public Hall.
29—West Kirby Cycling Club's Annual Dinner.
—West Kirby Orchestral Society's first Subscription Concert.

DECEMBER.

2—Starting of new Pumping Engine at the Water Works—Interesting ceremony and banquet.
6—Marriage of Miss Gertrude Cain to Mr. A. St. Clare Byrne.
7—Annual Meeting of the British and Foreign Bible Society.
8—Death of Mrs. Totty's dog "Sam."
9—Enthusiastic Meeting of North Ward Ratepayers—Mr. Tom Davies explains the Improvement Bill.
11—Wreck of the Hoylake fishing boat "Gipsy King" in Colwyn Bay.
12—Local Government Inquiry as to borrowing £2,000 for electric lighting.
13—Farmers and Tradesmen' Ball at Tynwald Hall, West Kirby.
14—The Improvement Bill passed the meeting of ratepayers.
15—District Council Meeting.
27—Grand Charity Concert for new Roman Catholic Presbytery, in Public Hall, West Kirby.
29—Annual Entertainment of Mostyn House School.

Chapter Four

Gifts to The Park

Improvements had been made to the lake by the following year as in July, 1902, an anonymous resident offered a free supply of water lilies. A further stock of fish was bought even though angling permits were refused on several occasions. Mr. Cummings MacDona, M.P., of Hilbre House, West Kirby, presented two swans for the lake in 1903. In addition to the two swans another one was acquired - a very handsome one, which was always referred to by the Stanley family as the Royal Swan as it was believed to have been obtained from Windsor Great Park. This swan, according to Mrs. Smith, for some reason had to go and it went to Eaton Hall, the Duke of Westminster's estate. As a child Lucy was told that it would be happier there as it had a real river to swim in. The swans were a problem in that they occasionally used to worry nervous ladies who walked by with their parasols. The ladies used to try and shoo them away or call at the Park Lodge and complain that a swan was walking about.

Another kind of incident Lucy Smith remembers from those Edwardian days was a nursemaid would report that a boy's toy yacht had been marooned in the middle of the lake. Usually it could not be rescued right away but there was a device of wires on a kind of set of pulleys which went across the lake, which her father and one of the men used (amongst other purposes) to rescue a toy yacht which got stranded in the middle of the lake.

Lucy Smith thinks that it was her father's suggestion that the lake was made, particularly she recollects a statement made by the Surveyor that "Mr. Stanley, from a swamp, had created a beautiful park". Certainly much of the ground in the Lower Park was rather swampy at the start. The lake is fed by streamlets draining into the lake underground. Mrs. Smith recollects that there was a Dr. Dempster who lived in Hilbre Road and there was a kind of drainage system running from his house into the lake.

Mr. Stanley was responsible for stocking the lake with ducks and other wild fowl. He bought Aylesbury and Muscovey ducks as well as mallards. In 1909 a Mr. Spelman of Clatterbridge gave a peacock to the Park. Mrs. Smith remembers that there were two peacocks but that the dogs used to go for these. In the same year it was decided to dispose of the three swans from the lake.

The Park and Church, West Kirby

Chapter Five

Permitted Pastimes

In the month of October, 1900 the first request for the provision of a public bowling green and tennis courts was made by Mr. G.I. Townsend of West Kirby but, due to the unsettled nature of the ground in the Lower Park, the plan was postponed. It was to be some time before the bowling green was finally established. A letter was read to the Committee from Miss E.H. Todd of Mostyn House School, 37 Church Road, West Kirby, in respect of tennis and croquet lawns in the Park but the Council felt unable to provide such lawns for private purposes. Quoiting grounds were set up but it appeared that the quoits must have been too expensive as the supply was returned and the framework of the quoiting pitches was removed immediately afterwards. The Council must have had second thoughts, however, as in 1904 the Surveyor was instructed to construct a quoiting ground in the Park. Mrs. Lucy Smith, one of the daughters of Mr. Stanley, recalls that 'her father was distinctly disapproving' over the proposal that quoits might be played in the Park. 'That game would be rather a come-down - lawn tennis and bowls were more proper and dignified pursuits in such a handsome park'. As late as 1912, however, the West Kirby Quoit Club asked for a reduction in the price of season tickets and for the provision of an additional quoiting bed in the Park. The latter was agreed but without the reduction in charge.

In 1904 it was agreed that two tennis courts be erected in the Lower Park, near Westbourne Grove, at a cost of £60. A Mr. G.W. Robins, on behalf of the newly-formed Brookfield Lawn Tennis Club was granted use of the courts on four days per week (including Saturday) at a rental of £20 per annum. By February 1905 two additional courts were made and in June dressing tents were erected for use of the members. The rent was increased to £45 per annum but reduced the following year to £40 on the understanding that the Club did not play on the days reserved for use of the general public. The Club was allowed to open on 15th May, 1905 but soon had to be reminded to leave the nets in position and to remove the dressing tents to the positions fixed by the Chairman of the Parks Committee and the Surveyor. The charge to the general public for tennis was 2d. per player for 1 set in 1906.

Little Lucy Stanley liked to go up to the tennis courts when she was four or five, pushing her doll's pram, watching the tennis and the tea parties which were a feature when the private club was in residence. There were sponge cakes and sandwiches being served at the tennis courts.

A few years earlier the Tennis Club had suggested that public courts be provided on the site of the old bowling green, which, presumably, was not up to standard at that time. This request was not agreed to, the reason being that the site was going to be devoted to croquet. In 1908 the Council went as far as inviting applications for partial use of the old bowling green in the Park for croquet but, as far as can be ascertained, this was not proceeded with.

It is evident that the Brookfield Lawn Tennis Club would have liked exclusive use of the tennis courts for there were frequent requests for this concession, which were always refused. The Parks Committee also refused to incur the expense of providing a permanent shelter and store for the Club in 1908.

Two private schools were allowed to use the courts in the 1908 and 1909 seasons - Miss Stephen's School and Springfield School. The Brookfield Lawn Tennis Club members continued to play on these courts in the Lower Park until 1910 when, although the charges were reduced to £30, the Secretary gave notice that they would not require the use of the courts for the next season.

It appears from the U.D.C. minutes that a bowling green was established in the Lower Park by 1905 but cannot have been up to the required standard for play, as in September of that year the Surveyor submitted estimates for enlarging and levelling the green at a cost of £150. Petitions were still coming in from ratepayers asking for a public bowling green and one was signed by 79 ratepayers in 1906 asking the Council to provide a suitable one in the Upper Park. This was agreed and the Upper Park bowling green was laid out by September, 1906, by George Washington of Fern Cottages, Market Street, Hoylake, at a cost of £149, It was not

The Bowling Green

taken over officially from the contractor until a year later.

The Upper Park bowling green was on part of the Glebe land so, naturally, Canon Blencowe from St. Bridget's Church, watched events closely. He enquired through his Solicitors on the laying out of the new green but was assured that the conditions of the lease had not been infringed. However, Canon Blencowe stipulated that the green should not be used for play or games on Sundays and asked that the Council restore it to its original condition at the end of the lease, if required.

One can imagine Canon Blencowe's distaste when in August, 1908, he had to make a further complaint regarding the erection of such an object as a urinal on the Bowling Green. The Parks Committee pointed out that it was only a temporary one for the convenience of the bowlers that season. After another letter was received they promised to remove the offending utility at the end of that time.

Two pavilions were built in the Park by November, 1906, at a cost of £50 each, and private lockers were provided too at a rental of 1/6d. per annum in 1908, reduced to 1/- (5p) per member the next year. Local joiners were invited to tender for shelters in the Park and the tender of J.W. Jackson, Hoylake, was accepted for two shelters at a cost of £68. 7s.0d. Charges made to members of the West Kirby Bowling Club in 1906 were 4/- per season, 5/- (25p) for non-members.

The Park, West Kirby

Chapter Six
Vandalism

Vandalism is nothing new as the Park-keeper reported several infringements of the Byelaws and the Law Clerk was instructed to caution offenders. The Surveyor was empowered to order a dozen notice plates requesting visitors to 'keep off the grass' and additional notice plates were to be fixed in the Park to assist in protecting trees, shrubs and flowers. A report was received of damage to shrubs, and letters were written to the parents of the boys concerned. During the summer Mr. Stanley was granted extra help for a period of two weeks and on another occasion for a month.

Lucy, his daughter, says her father had to be very vigilant over the bowling green because, despite the notices to 'keep off the grass" children would take short cuts across, particularly children going to St. Bridget's School. There still are concrete steps (now sealed up) leading to the railway bridge by Church Road. Children would cut across the bowling green and go up these steps instead of going round the road. Mr. Stanley had to make a point of being there when children were going to and fro to school to head them off the bowling green, which had to be kept in immaculate condition.

Generally, there did not appear to be any real nastiness and Mrs. Smith remembers children enjoyed such simple pleasures as standing on the railway bridge and getting drenched with smoke and steam (which their mothers did not like) while the train passed underneath.

Chapter Seven

Wages and Working Conditions

Mr. Stanley, the Park-keeper, applied for an increase in wages in 1902 and 1904, which were refused. He was finally granted an increase to 27s. 6d. (£1.37p) per week in February, 1905 'with house clear, and fuel and light provided'.

Although the wages appear very small by modern standards, the cost of living then compared favourably with the present. In 1900, Mr. Jones, a dairyman in Cable Road, Hoylake, was advertising a quart (2 pints) of milk at 3 old pence, delivered daily. Mr. W. Eccles of The Stores, Hoylake, was selling a loaf of bread for 3 old pence and eggs were 12 for 1/- (5p). Butter and tea were both 1/- per lb. in 1901.

Clothes were more expensive as follows:-

Youths Overcoats:	12s. 6d.	Norfolk Suit:	5s. 0d.
Boys Overcoats:	7s. 6d.	Velvet Suit:	4s. 11d.
Infants Overcoats:	5s. 0d.	Cardigan:	5s. 0d.
Singlet and drawers:	5s. 0d.		
Vicuna cloth overcoat:	21s. 0d.		

House prices in 1900 were between £275 - £300 in Westbourne Grove, West Kirby, but the majority of residents would rent property in those days at a rent of a few shillings per week.

Conditions were slowly improving for Council employees. Workmen were allowed two days' holiday with full pay on the 26th and 27th June, 1902, for the Coronation Celebrations (Edward VII). This perhaps was an exception but in 1907 the Council granted one week's holiday, with full pay, to those workmen in employ of the General Purposes and Parks Committee who had had one year's continuous service. In 1910 sick pay was granted at the rate of 8/- per week to any workman who had been in the continuous employ of the Council for at least 12 months preceding the absence. The workman had to supply a medical certificate to cover his illness (other than absence through injury which was covered by the Workman's Compensation Acts), and payment was limited to a period not exceeding 13 weeks. It was suggested that a meeting between Councillors and representatives of workmen be arranged with a view to establishing a permanent sick fund to be managed by the workmen themselves.

Chapter Eight

The Social Scene

The Upper Park was used for various activities up to the First World War. Mr. Emil Gipprich, a 'gentleman' living at Ferndine, Banks Road. was granted permission for the use of the park for the children's entertainment in connection with the Coronation Celebrations (Edward VII) 1902. The following year Mr. Gipprich, as Honorary Secretary of West Kirby District Band, offered to give performances in the Park, provided the Council erected a suitable band stand. Temporary wood flooring was laid and the Surveyor was asked to supply seats during band performances in the park.

In 1905 the Parks and Gardens Committee gave permission for the West Kirby Carnival Committee to hold their annual fete on the top field. At this time there were paths but a certain amount of it was rough meadow. According to Mrs. Lucy Smith, the last surviving daughter of Mr. Stanley, the part of the Upper Park towards Grange Road, was always known as the far field and the middle stretch as the meadow. The grass on the rough meadow had to be cut with scythes, the hay was stacked, and this was donated to local donkey owners, particularly those who took parties across to Hilbre Island. One of the firms which took hay away was run by a man called Jim Lawrence. Mrs. Smith remembers Mr. Lawrence and his sister pitchforking the hay into a wagon. There was also a fairly sizeable pond with bulrushes and kingcups (of which there is now no trace) in front of the present bowling green in the Top Park.

In 1910 the Secretary of the West Kirby and Hoylake Flower Show asked to use the upper portion of the Park for a flower show and children's sports to be held in July. Mr. Stanley's daughter Lucy recalls that this was an annual event with an entrance fee of six old pence. She remembers with pride and pleasure as she was an exhibitor on several occasions. She exhibited little bunches of wild flowers and grasses and, although never winning a first prize, she gained a second or third prize on more than one occasion. Her father was on the Committee which helped to organise the flower show.

A Mr. Charles Leicester applied to place rowing boats for hire on the Park lake the same summer but that was firmly rejected.

In West Kirby itself and Hoylake there had been great rejoicings on May 26th, 1900, at the relief of Mafeking. Rockets went off, people streamed from their houses to demonstrate their joy. There were processions and bands in the streets. On the Banks Road/Ashton Drive spare land, bonfires were lit and effigies of Kruger burnt. Flags hung from windows and the shops closed on the Monday.

Shop hours were long in those days. They closed at 7 p.m. on four evenings (Monday - Thursday), 8 p.m. on a Friday and 10 p.m. on Saturday. There was an Early Closing Movement locally in 1899, the suggestion being that the shops should close on Wednesdays at 4 p.m. Although at first there was opposition to this by some shopkeepers, it was eventually agreed.

Lucy Smith remembers that in the Upper Park there was a band stand, which was situated on a little rise straight ahead from the railway bridge. Visiting bands used to play and included a number of German bands, which were a great feature of life in Edwardian days. One of these was Herr Adam Groupe of Southport who was given permission to hold band performances in the streets for three months from January to March, 1901. He was still visiting the district ten years later when there was a recommendation from the Parks and Gardens Committee that a gramophone recital might be held in the Park and the public gardens. The offer was referred to Herr Groupe (or to some suitable tradesman) and it was suggested that a trial concert be allowed in each place. What became of this idea is not known.

For the Coronation Festivities in 1911 the Council arranged tea and entertainment for children between 4 and 15 years of age at a cost of 1s.3d. per head. Souvenirs in the form of medals or brooches were to be

Rose Cummins and her trap at Hilbre Island

Going to the Flower Show in the Top Park

supplied to children residing in the district at a cost not exceeding 3d. each. Tea and entertainment was also given to residents aged 65 and upwards at an estimated total cost of £20. The District Band was hired to play in the Parade Gardens in Hoylake at a cost of £2 and the Children's Entertainment Committee were empowered to engage a band for West Kirby on similar terms.

Chapter Nine

Mr. Foster's Folly

Thomas Foster who played such an important part in the development of the district was appointed as Surveyor in June, 1894 at a salary of £78 per annum. He was also appointed Inspector of Nuisances at the same time at a salary of £100 per annum. As Inspector of Nuisances he would have had to deal with complaints from the public regarding annoyances, obstructions and encroachments. The section of the Birkenhead News reporting on West Kirby and Hoylake in 1901 mentions visitors then were complaining they were being kept awake by cocks crowing, dogs barking and cats fighting. There was also a complaint in August 1901 of a dung heap piled high against the back wall of a tenanted house in Hoylake. It also referred to the fact that many houses lacked modern sanitary conveniences and that cess pools were still in use.

In the ten years that he was with the Council Mr. Foster had huge responsibilities for he undertook, on very tight budgets, the building of the promenades in Hoylake and West Kirby, the Marine Lake with the boathouse and slipways, roads, boulevards and gardens, as well as drawing up plans and tenders for the construction of the Park. In 1896 his salaries for these jobs were increased to £110 and £140 respectively. He was highly thought of by the majority of the Councillors but was occasionally criticised by a few and quite unfairly by a member of the Press.

A Mr. Frederick May from Hoylake wrote for the Herald and Visitor under the nom de plume of "Spectator". In his articles he had cast doubts on Mr. Foster's competence as an engineer on the dredging of the Marine Lake, the increased cost of construction, and queried the payment of a bonus to him by the Council. These jibes led the respected Surveyor into an unfortunate incident and a subsequent appearance in Court. On the 3rd October, 1901, Mr. Foster met Mr. May out walking with his   brother-in-law across the sandhills from Birkenhead Road, between Hoylake and Meols.

Mr. Foster had approached Mr. May and said: "Are you the person who has been making remarks about my ability as an engineer?" Mr. May had replied "If you will make your question clearer I think I shall be able to satisfy you". Mr. Foster went on "Are you the person who writes under the name of 'Spectator' in the Herald?" Mr. May responded "I think you had better see the editor and ask him the name of his correspondent". Mr. Foster angrily retorted "I have seen him. I asked him yesterday and he told me it is you, and that is my way of dealing with you". With that Mr. Foster lost control and aimed a blow at the left side of Mr. May's face, missed and knocked off his hat. Mr. Foster followed with another blow, which struck Mr. May in the eye, breaking his spectacles. May's brother-in-law intervened but was told by Mr. Foster it was no affair of his. Mr. May then said to his brother-in-law "Leave him alone. I will deal with him in a different way" and Mr. Foster retorted "You have got your witnesses and you can do what you like."

At the resulting Court case Thomas Foster was fined 40s. with costs. He subsequently apologised to the District Council, saying that he had acted under great provocation caused by repeated and unfounded attacks which had been made on him in the public press. He now recognised that his proper course of action, as the attacks had been made in connection with work he had done for the Council as their servant, should have been to submit the matter to the Council. He expressed his regret for not having taken this step in the first instance.

Mr. Ellison, one of the Councillors, in proposing the Council's continued and unabated confidence in Mr. Foster's ability, remarked that, even though the original estimate for the Marine Lake had been £2,500 , the many additions were made by order of the Council and the cost had not reached the £5,000 stated by Mr. May. The Chairman, Mr. George Wall, supported the resolution as to Mr. Foster's integrity and ability, which had been seconded by Mr. Clare. Mr. Foster's salary was raised to £300 per annum as Surveyor in 1903, fixed at £350 for the following year and afterwards at a rate of £400 per annum maximum. He remained a loyal servant of the Council until 1904 when he resigned to go into private practice but offered his services as Consulting Engineer.

A suggestion by Mr. Griffiths, one of the Councillors, that a testimonial be given to Mr. Foster on leaving was met with petty mindedness by the Chairman, J. Fergus Smith, who disagreed 'because of a personal matter.' When pressed he said 'He had not liked the way Mr. Foster had treated him in front of the Town Hall when he had asked Mr. Foster to allow a gardener into the Park Lodge that the Surveyor had built, before Mr. Foster thought it was ready and Mr. Foster had said he would wash his hands of it'. This was obviously when Mr. Stanley was appointed to Ashton Park.

Chapter Ten

Problems for the Park-Keeper

Bowling greens are difficult to maintain in a pristine condition and their maintenance caused problems between, on the one hand, the Parks Committee and the Surveyor who acted on their behalf, and on the other Mr. Stanley, the Park-keeper, and his men. Not only was Mr. Stanley looking after the Park but he was responsible for the maintenance of the boulevards and street gardens and verges. In 1907 it was agreed that his duties be confined to West Kirby Park. He had two assistants at this time Joseph Parry and James Devlin. In 1908 Mr. Stanley applied for further assistance in West Kirby Park. The Park Committee's answer was to arrange for the Chairman and Surveyor to draw up a working scheme for the guidance of the Park-keeper, that the Park-keeper's attention be called to the unsatisfactory state of the grounds at present and that he be required to work under the control and supervision of the Surveyor. At this particular time Joseph Parry had finished working in the Park and it was agreed that James Wells should succeed him.

An incident was reported to the Parks Committee the following month when, in a letter, a Captain Thornber of West Kirby, complained on behalf of his wife of the action of the Park-keeper in connection with their dog straying in the Park. A report was read from Mr. Stanley and his explanation accepted. Reading between the lines of the formal minutes it would seem that Mrs. Thornber's excuse was that she did not realise Mr. Stanley was acting in his official capacity as Park-keeper over the matter of her dog straying as he was not wearing a uniform, hence the outcome that the Council decided that the Park-keeper and his assistants should wear uniform hats when on duty.

The Bowling Match

It was not unheard of for Park employees to wear uniform as it was already in force at Birkenhead Park. In 1894 the Park-keeper there is recorded as wearing a £5 uniform of blue coat and trousers, scarlet vest and cap with cover. In 1899 similar resplendent articles of uniform were ordered for the park watchmen at Birkenhead. Mr. Stanley, however, was a spirited and forthright man and he wrote back to the Council in no uncertain manner. The Committee bluntly resolved:-

"That the Park-keeper be requested to wear the hat provided by the Council or send in his resignation." [8]

Mr. Stanley presumably complied with the request for he is not mentioned again in the Park Committee minutes until the following April (1909) when the Chairman and another Councillor were empowered to enquire into the neglected condition of the bowling green in West Kirby Park and asked to report back. They were also empowered to give such instructions with regard to maintenance and management of greens as they might deem advisable.

In October, 1909, a sub-committee was appointed to inspect and report on the condition of the bowling green in the Upper Park and a recommendation was made that the turf be removed and replaced by turf from the site of the old bowling green in the Lower Park, the latter green to be sown with grass seed. Progress was monitored and in January, 1910 the Engineer and Surveyor (Mr. Fraser) received instructions as to sowing of the old bowling green and to maintenance of the new green in the upper grounds.

In July, 1910, the Parks Committee considered an extract from the report of the Park-keeper (J. Stanley) as to the supervision of the Park bowling green, in which he objected to the arrangements made by the Engineer and Surveyor for the weekly inspection of the green. The Committee resolved:-

> "That the Engineer and Surveyor be instructed to find employment for Stanley outside the Park for a period of 3 months, at his present salary, and that his duties be reconsidered at the end of that period." [9]

At the end of that period the Parks and Gardens Committee submitted their recommendations to the General Purposes and Parliamentary Committee, which were considered by that body along with correspondence from Mr. Stanley. At the meeting held on 18th October, 1910, it was resolved:-

> "That the correspondence be approved and, that in accordance therewith, Stanley be now engaged as working foreman in the Park, under the direction and control of the Engineer and Surveyor, and that his wages be now fixed at 27/6d. per week. with house, fuel and light provided." [10]

Matters came to a head in May, 1911, when the Engineer and Surveyor submitted reports from employees engaged in West Kirby Park. A Sub-Committee was appointed to investigate the reports and the complaints of the Foreman and to report generally on the management of the Park. After investigations the Sub-Committee recommended that

(i) J.J. Stanley to be removed from the Park and to take up the duties of E. Hadwin on the boulevards and gardens at a remuneration of 30/- per week;

(ii) E. Hadwin to be appointed Working Foreman in place of Stanley in the Park at a remuneration of 25/- per week with park house (free and fuel and light provided). [11]

Of the other gardeners William Smith stayed on in the Park at his present wages, William Rutter was found other employement with the Council by the Engineer and Surveyor, and a Fred Parr was transferred to the Park at a remuneration of 17/- per week. The Council expressed their confidence and satisfaction in the conduct of the Engineer and Surveyor in relation to the Park at West Kirby.

As Lucy Smith, his daughter, recalls, the Council were loath to part with Mr. Stanley's services. According to Mrs. Smith he improved a run-down garden in Hoylake known as the Quadrant Garden behind the Town Hall, as well as looking after the grass verges and the boulevards, as Meols Drive was known. He was also consulted about the Parade Gardens in Hoylake where, apparently, the Council were having trouble because nothing would grow, understandably, in the sandy soil. He recommended that a sunken garden be created and this flourished.

According to the family, Mr. Stanley remained on the Council force until war broke out in August 1914, when he enlisted in the army. He had been in the volunteer reserves. Mr. Stanley never saw service at the front but remained in the army for the whole of the First World War. He did not return to the service of the Council.

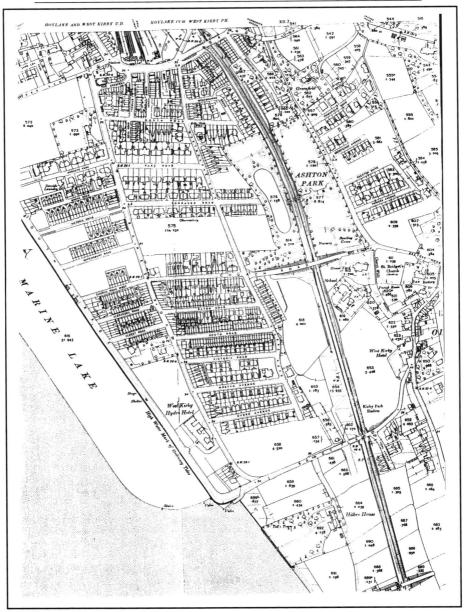

Map of West Kirby (section) 1911

Chapter Eleven

The Second Park-Keeper

Edward Hadwin, the second Park-keeper, was born in Cark in Cartmel, near Grange-over-Sands. He came to Wirral in his early twenties towards the end of the last century, sailing round from Morecambe Bay to Hoylake with several other young men in their nobby for the fishing, which was good at Hoylake in those days.

It is believed that Mr. Hadwin started working for the Council when the promenades were being built and that he became a 'ganger' or foreman because of his organising abilities. He had been working as a gardener on the boulevards and gardens before he was transferred to Ashton Park as Working Foreman in 1911. He must have been helped in those early days by his brother who was Head Gardener for the Cavendishes of Holker Hall. He was given the tenancy of the Park Lodge with his young family.

The author has recalled her memories of her grandfather, the Lodge and the Park:-

'As a child I absolutely adored my Grandad. I know now, having spoken to my sister, brothers and cousins, that he had this effect on all his grandchildren, particularly of making a child feel special.

I can first remember sitting on his knee and his teasingly brushing my cheek with his white moustache. It was, I noticed with that clarity of childhood, tinged with a brownish tea stain at the edges.

Edward Hadwin, the second Park-Keeper,
with his family - Henry, Annie (his wife), Edward
holding John, Tom

I slid off his knee and he laughingly asked "Getting too big for sitting on my knee then?" I blushed a firey red but would not get on again. He would sit in his easy chair by the fire and take his boots off. His trouser legs were tied at the bottom with string the mark of his trade - for he was a gardener, not any ordinary gardener but the Park-keeper of Ashton Park, West Kirby. He actually supervised the work of all the parks and gardens for the Hoylake Urban District Council and lived in the Park Lodge.

Whenever I visited the Park Lodge I did not see my Grandfather reading anything except a gardening book or his Bible. He was a

42

devout Christian and attended the Presbyterian Church. He also used to write poetry, which he kept rolled up in a large chest of drawers.

I loved visiting my Grandparents at the Park Lodge. I can still see the house in my mind's eye with its formal round and half-moon flower beds with the slender short railings surrounding the front lawn. A parlour overlooked these. A front door (which was never used by us children) led into the hall, from which was the front parlour with the kitchen behind. A walk-in pantry led off the kitchen where Grandma kept her preserves and groceries and put her baking and puddings to cool. The back door opened onto a yard, at the side of which were several small out buildings. In one was kept the corn for the hens. It was not unusual to see a hen or two hanging upside down in the next. Grandad would boil all the old vegetable peelings in a galvanised bucket on the stove. "Do you want a bit then?" he would say and proffer a spoonful on a metal spoon. At other times when I would go round it would be cockles boiling briskly on the stove. I could never take to those but Grandad enjoyed still his trips to Hilbre Island to gather cockles.

I revelled in the beauty of the park. The crocuses at the side of the house delighted me. There used to be a little path which led to the back of the house, with a fountain on the corner leading to public toilets. On one side Grandad had built an Anderson Shelter in the Second World War but afterwards grew mushrooms in it. It was there that he fell down once and broke his leg. The greenhouses were opposite the back yard. I'm sure I gained my love of gardening by endlessly following my Grandad round, watching him tending his geraniums and tomatoes and damping down the glass houses. The smell of humid heat intermingled with the astringent scent of geraniums and tomatoes, brings the memory back instantly. "But, why are you doing that Grandad?" I used to say as I followed like a little shadow behind him. The bay tree still grows in the Park and, even now, I cannot resist taking a leaf and crushing it in my hands to appreciate its aroma. The 'fairy' bower I remember too - a trellis or pergola hanging with honeysuckle and a   tangle of roses.

The bowling greens were my Grandad's pride and joy, also the grass tennis courts in the top park. On the lake he had his ducks

The Fairy Bower

and sometimes I used to help hold one side of the long rope to gather them in for the night into their secure pens. There was no island in the middle of the lake in those days.

As I grew older and was allowed to play with other children in the park, I, being a bit of a tomboy, loved climbing trees. You can imagine my alarm if there was a shout of "Parkie" and away we would rush off. I knew I had to run faster than anyone else in case my Grandfather should spot me amongst the fleeing children.

I remember being caught one time by Mr. Fahy, our neighbour and the confectioner, who saw me walking across the **outside** of the railway bridge - a highly dangerous practice! I did get a telling off when I reached home that day! In my teens I was once dared by my friends to walk through the Park in the dark on my own, which I did. My heart thumped wildly but all I heard were murmurings of the 'lovebirds' in the shelters. I can also remember walking back through the Park one moonlight night after a dance at the Blenheim with my boy friend (my future husband). I was wearing a pale blue long dress. All very romantic but my husband cannot remember the occasion!

I've since pushed my children in their prams through the Park to play on the swings and now, in retirement, get just as much pleasure from taking my young grand children to the playground and to feed the ducks on the lake. I have so many happy memories, particularly of my Grandfather and perhaps you can see why I appreciate Ashton Park so very much.'

Edward Hadwin with wife Annie and young relative

Chapter Twelve
Borders, Beds, Shrubs and Trees

In the minutes of the Parks and Gardens Committee covering the early years of the Park, mention is made of plants which have been purchased:-

bulbs £3.00; plants, seeds and rose trees £3.2s.7d.. young trees £3. 7s. 6d; these being ordered by Mr. Stanley, and the main planting of trees by Dickson's of Chester, at a cost of £65.19s.0d.

It is aggravating, however, that records have not been kept of the varieties bought, so the following details have been gleaned from various sources.

In municipal parks at the turn of the century carpet bedding was popular in a variety of forms. There used to be half moon as well as round beds in front of the Park Lodge. This early photo (1906/07) shows a display of tulips edged with pelargoniums. Lucy is standing in the doorway. The beds also used to be edged with rosettes of succulents with light green to grey leaves.

In an old gardening book of Mr. Hadwin's (Beeton's Dictionary of Everyday Gardening) he has listed some of the packets of seeds he bought, so it is known that he grew 10 week stocks, dwarf Victoria Asters, giant Japanese Comet, Verbena Defiance, Shirley Poppies (mixed colours), single Petunias, Crystal Palace and White Gem Lobelia and White Pearl Godetia. There is a diagram of a Spring bed of red tulips, forget-me-nots, aquilegias, edged with yellow and white violas. The author remembers purple, white and yellow crocuses under a tree at the side of the Lodge. Mrs. Dolly Shipman one of the three girls taken on in the First World War recalls that, with Mr. Hadwin, she planted bedding plants in the Lower Park such as the shrubby calceolarias, pansies and the red tinted daises (bellis perennis).

There were the common fuchias and shrubs such as laurels, red flowering currant, glossy leaved mahonia, contoneasters, buddleia, golden forsythia. pink hydrangeas, sweet scented Philadelphus, plain and variegated hollies, privet, lilac and many others.

The older trees in the Park, which have been identified by a landscape gardener, are varied and consist of -

Lower Park Playground area and field:-

 Oak (quercus robur)
 Common Sycamore (Acer pseudo platanus)
 Holly (Ilex aquifolium)
 Copper Beech (Fagus purpurea)
 Red Pine (Pinus resinosa)
 Lombardy Poplar (Populus fastigiata)
 Beech (Fagus sylvatica)
 Lime (Tilia Europaea)
 English Elm (Ulnus procera)
 Ash (Fraxinus excelsior)
 Crack Willow (Salix fragilis)
 Holm Oak (Quercus ilex) an evergreen with its tiny acorns
 Hawthorn (Crataegus monogyna)

On the field itself is a magnificent London Plane tree (Platanus acerifolia).

At the lakeside are an old laburnum, spotted laurel, castor oil plant, lombardy poplar, oak, beech, horse chestnut and an interesting Swamp Cypress (taxudium distichum), Scots Pine (pinus sylvestris) and a Whitebeam (Pyrus aria) known as the poorman's magnolia.

At the far side of the Lower Park bowling green is a fine vista of trees, including euonymus (Spindle tree), horse chestnut, several palms, an Atlantic blue cedar (cedrus Atlantica), and a Monkey Puzzle tree or Chile Pine (Araucaria araucana), so called because it is said to be the only tree the monkey cannot climb due to the sharp, stiff leaves armed with thorns. The Monkey Puzzle tree is thought to have come from Holker Hall, near Cartmel, where Mr. Hadwin's brother was Head Gardener.

Amongst the trees on the right-hand side path leading to the Lodge from the bowling green there is an aromatic bay tree (laurus nobilis), tulip tree (liriodendron tulipiera) which flowers about every 25 years, a European larch (laurix decidua) and a euonymus (Spindle tree).

In the top park, trees of particular interest are a majestic Monterey Cypress (Cupressus macrocarpa) by the bowling green, which grows faster in Britain, particularly on the South coast, than in its native California. There is also a weeping silver birch (betula pendula). Dolly Shipman recalls that when she and Mr. Hadwin pruned the trees in the top park two rather eccentric elderly ladies from Carpenter's Lane used to sit in the Park and cry!

WILD LIFE AND FLOWERS

The Ranger responsible for the Park to-day has recorded 45 species of birds, ranging from the more common blackbird, thrush, starling, sparrow, robin, tits (Great, Blue, Coal and Willow), wren, chaffinch, doves, pigeons, magpies, finches, etc. to the rarer winter visitors such as redwings and fieldfares.

On the lake at present are moorhens, Canada geese and mallards, together with visiting sea birds - the blackheaded and herring gulls. The Little Grebe and Goldeneye Duck are only seen rarely in extreme weather conditions.

The squirrels one sees in the trees have only taken up residence in recent times.

In the more natural and quieter corners of the Park there is a variety of wild flowers, including foxgloves, red campion and the lesser celandine.

ADVERTISEMENTS.   v

BARR'S SUPERIOR SEEDS
FOR FLOWER & KITCHEN GARDEN

BARR'S SEED GUIDE (free) contains a Select List of the best Seeds for securing a supply of Vegetables "The Year Round," and a full Descriptive List of the most beautiful Annuals and Perennials for keeping the Flower Garden and Greenhouse always gay. It is full of practical Hints on the culture of Vegetables and Flowers, valuable to Gardeners, Amateurs and Exhibitors.

Barr's Collections of Vegetable Seeds,
5/6, 7/6, 12/6, 21/-, 42/-, 63/- to 105/-.

Barr's Collections of Choice Flower Seeds,
2/6, 5/6, 7/6, 10/6, 15/-, 21/-, 30/-, 42/-, 63/-.

Full particulars on application.

BARR'S BEAUTIFUL HARDY DAFFODILS
GOLD MEDAL
THE MOST LOVELY OF ALL SPRING FLOWERS

Barr's Daffodils were awarded the only Gold Medal at the Royal Horticultural Society's First Great Daffodil Conference, 1884; Premier Prize, 1894; Gold Medal, 1896; Gold Medal, 1899; Two Gold Medals, First Prize, and £10 10s. Challenge Cup, 1901; Two Gold Medals, 1902; Gold Medal, 1903; Gold Medal, 1904; Gold Medal, 1905; Two Gold Medals, 1906; Two Gold Medals, 1907; and Five Gold Medals, 1908.

Barr's 21/- Amateur's Collection of Daffodils contains 6 Bulbs each of 26 high-class Daffodils, suitable for the Greenhouse or Select Flower Border.

Barr's 21/- "Woodland" Collection of Daffodils contains 500 Bulbs in 20 fine showy varieties, suitable for naturalising in Grass, Shrubberies, etc.

Barr's Collections of Bulbs,
For Indoors and Outdoors,

Barr's 21/- "Greenhouse" Collection contains 300 Spring-flowering Bulbs, of finest quality.

Barr's 21/- "Flower Garden" Collection contains 600 Spring and Summer-flowering Bulbs, all decorative.

Barr's 21/- "Woodland" Collection contains 800 Bulbs suitable to naturalise in Woodlands, Orchards, Wild Gardens, etc.

For full particulars of the above and other Collections, see Barr's Bulb Catalogue.

BARR & SONS, 11, 12, & 13, KING ST., LONDON.
COVENT GARDEN,
Nurseries: SURBITON, SURREY.   Visitors invited.

Two Views of Top Park

Telephone 2777.

T. TOTTY,

FRUITERER AND FLORIST,

ALSO

Grower and Retailer of Vegetables.

Choice Selection of English & Foreign Fruits.

Wreaths, Sprays, &c., made to order,

VEGETABLES FRESH CUT DAILY.

Potatoes a Speciality.

48, MARKET STREET, HOYLAKE;

Avondale Buildings, Banks Road ;

28, GRANGE ROAD, WEST KIRBY.

The doctor says—"That a little fruit taken before breakfast is one of the best means of regulating the system."

Ring o' Bells Hotel,

WEST KIRBY, CHESHIRE.

This Hotel is most delightfully situated in the most healthy and picturesque part of West Kirby, and within three minutes' walk from the New Station of the L. and N. W. and G. W. Joint Railways (Kirby Park), and ten minutes' from the terminus of the Mersey and Wirral Railways. The shore is also within a few minutes' easy walking distance, and a ramble on the celebrated hills may be commenced from the very door.

A new Bowling Green has been recently added, situated in the most picturesque position, with delightful views of the surrounding country.

GOOD ACCOMMODATION AND A LIBERAL TABLE.

Moderate Charges. Tariff on application.

DINNER, PIC-NIC PARTIES, &c., SPECIALLY CATERED FOR.
ESTIMATES FREE.

EXCELLENT STABLING.   BILLIARDS.   BOWLS.

THOMAS LOWE,
Proprietor.

Week-End Tariff,
15/- to 21/-.

51

Chapter Thirteen

The Park in the First World War

With the coming of the 1st World War everything changed, nothing would ever be the same again.

Conscription was not brought in at first but Council employees were allowed to enlist (except two employees at the Electric Lighting Works). These two men could go if they so desired if the Engineer and Surveyor could arrange replacements. The Council employees had to enlist before 11th December, 1915 in order to get a supplement to their forces pay. An application was made later in 1916 by the Engineer and Surveyor, on behalf of John McLelland, the horse-keeper, for exemption from military service. There is no record if permission was given.

When the men were called up Dolly Rutter was the first girl gardener of three to be taken on in the Park. She had been working at Biddles, the market gardeners in Moreton, at 4°d. per hour, and was well used to hard work. She worked in the Park with Mr. Hadwin whom she describes as 'a lovely man' with whom she never had a cross word.

As early as 1912 a scheme was drawn up by the Council for providing allotments in the upper grounds of the Park in West Kirby. The Clerk was asked to apply for the appropriation of the site for that purpose. In 1916 a Cultivation of Lands Order was brought in and for Hoylake Urban District Council a schedule was prepared of unoccupied lands and names of residents and societies desirous of cultivating land. 45 applications for allotments were received and 6 tons of seed potatoes were ordered by the Council. The Engineer and Surveyor was empowered to terminate the existing arrangements with Thomas Totty as to purchase of street sweepings. In March the Chairman of the Cultivation of Lands Committee reported that the number of allotments taken from the Council to date were 52 in West Kirby, 81 in Hoylake, 15 in Meols and, in addition, 30 approximately from the Railway Company.

There were allotments in Proctor Road, Gorse Road, the Park and on Grange Hill. Tennis Court No. 2 was requested as an additional allotment. In October 1917 it was agreed that:-

1. A barricade be fixed to prevent trespass on the Park Allotments from Mr. Christian's land;

2. A passage be made to enable manure to be carried on to the Park Allotments, and

3. The Engineer and Surveyor communicate with the Rev. Canon Blencowe with reference to land in his possession suitable for allotments.

In 1917 Mr. Maitland, the Assistant Surveyor, joined the Army. Joe Parry, who had worked in the Park at one time, was sadly killed in the War.

Chapter Fourteen

The Park Today

Ashton Park has undergone many changes over the years. The tennis courts in the Lower Park were replaced, probably between the wars, by the children's playground. The writer remembers as a small child in the late 30s playing there and the feeling of unfairness she felt because the swings were tied up on Sundays whilst grown-ups could play on the golf courses if they wished.

The Victoria Bowling Club is a longstanding one and derives its name from the fact that its members had to play in the Victoria Gardens on the South Parade at the end of the 1st World War as the bowling green in the Park was being used for concert parties, complete with stage and seats. Mr. Fred Ibbotson (aged 91 and an active player still) remembers returning to play on the present green in 1921/2. Today the Victoria Bowling Club in the lower park is still thriving with a membership of 40.

The Upper Park bowling green established in 1906 has a men's team in the morning and the ladies play in the afternoon. The Ladies Club was founded in 1928/29 with the encouragement of Mr. Edward Case who donated a cup "The Charlotte Case" cup after his wife, which is still played for today. They have an active membership of over 40 and play 3 teams in the Birkenhead and District Ladies League.

The West Kirby to Hooton branch railway line, which separates the Lower and Upper Parks, ran its last official passenger train in 1956, closing finally to freight trains (as well as the occasional passenger traffic) in 1962. In 1964 began the removal of this railway system and the route soon became wild and derelict. Part of the land was even acquired for

The Wirral Way (W.S. Williams)

The Model Boat Club (M. Friend)

housing development but, fortunately, there were people who were concerned over the loss of Wirral's countryside and footpaths and came up with the idea of converting the line to a Country Park, the first one in Britain, in 1969. The Wirral Country Park, or Wirral Way as the old railway line is known, is used extensively by the public and is easily accessible from the Park for extended walks.

There used to be a First World War tank situated on the old bandstand area but this disappeared. Was it taken for munitions in the Second World War?

Miss Ashton died in 1935, and in 1937 the Council purchased her land used for the park for the sum of £3950. The lease for the Glebe land is now coming to its end.

In the past the park was used, not only for local competitions, but for prestigious Tennis Championships with such famous players as Boris Becker and John McEnroe. As part of the Ashton Park centenary celebrations a tennis tournament was held in the summer of 1996 through a European grant, matched by funds from the Local Authority.

The Wirral Model Boat Club was formed in 1981 by five enthusiasts. Before the park lake could be used it had to be cleared of weeds and these still build up from time to time but is only of minimal hindrance to the enjoyment of the members. The Club has grown from strength to strength since those early days. It holds various regattas throughout the year, namely Tug Towing, Scale Steering and '575' Yachts. Members' interests in model boating are very varied and they take pride in exhibiting their skills and boats at outside events as well as on the park lake. There is a Junior section too.

On the 31st May, 1991 the "Friends of Ashton Park" came into existence with the following aims:-

(a) To be a responsible body to protect the park and its wildlife and to seek the maintenance and improvement of its facilities for the benefit of the residents of West Kirby, park users and the general public. To encourage Wirral Borough Council to promote investment to improve toilets, sporting facilities, footpaths, benches and fencing.

(b) To educate the public in the history and other aspects of the park.

(c) To accept donations, grants and subscriptions to be used specifically for the further improvement of the park.

Several events were held in the park during the celebratory year of 1996, including a May Fair and in June/July a week of entertainment with local societies taking part. A medallion was also struck to mark the Centenary Year (as shown on the back cover). An exhibition showing photographs and the history of the park was held in the Concourse Library, West Kirby, during October.

The Park-keeper has been replaced by Wirral Country Park Rangers who patrol regularly and who are involved with the management of the park. They also work closely with the 'Friends' group to safeguard the future of Ashton Park. Anyone interested in becoming a 'Friend' should contact Wirral Country Park, Thurstaston (Tel: 0151 648 4371) for further details.

In 1902 one of the Councillors declared that Ashton Park was 'not a necessity after all, it was merely a luxury' but the many residents and visitors who use the park today would certainly disagree. It is a valued amenity and is a tribute to the work of those early Surveyors, Councillors, Park-keepers and gardeners who, despite all the difficulties and delays experienced in establishing the Park, have left this delightful legacy, 'a little oasis', for us to enjoy now and in future years.

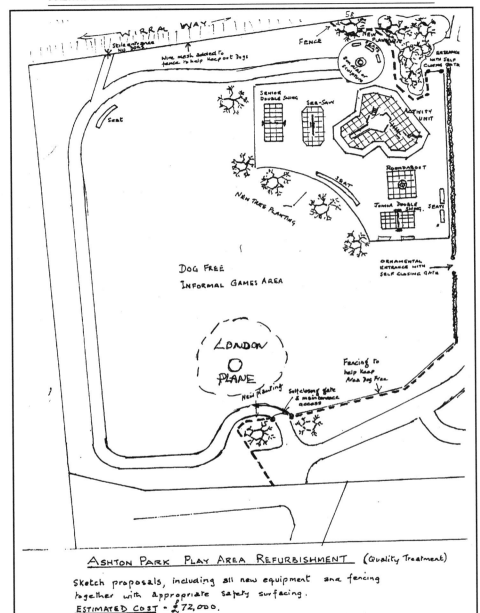

ASHTON PARK PLAY AREA REFURBISHMENT (Quality Treatment)

Sketch proposals, including all new equipment and fencing
together with appropriate safety surfacing.
ESTIMATED COST - £72,000.

Appendix

WAGES OF COUNCIL WORKMEN
- SEPTEMBER, 1913

Bin Scavengers   Increase from 24/- to 25/- per week

Horse Drivers   Increase from 24/- to 25/- per week with
                        further advance of 1/- per week on
                        completion of 2 years' service.

Sewer Men   Increase from 5°d. and 6d. per hour to
                        6d and 6°d. per hour

Ordinary Labourers   Increase from 5°d. per hour to 6d. per
                        hour as determined by the Engineer and
                        Surveyor

Gangers   Increase from 6°d. to 7d. per hour

SALARIES OF COUNCIL WORKERS
- OCTOBER 1913

R.W. Fraser, Engineer and Surveyor	Present salary maximum £350 per annum. Increase to £400 maximum to be attained in 5 annual increments of £10 from 1st April, 1914
H. Maitland, Assistant Surveyor and Building Inspector	Present joint salary £160 per annum. Maximum to be increased from £160 to £175 per annum by 2 annual increments of £7. 10s. 0d. - from 1st April, 1914
A.B. Brown, Clerk to Engineer and Surveyor and Building Inspector	Present salary £145 per annum maximum. Increase to £165 per annum maximum by 4 annual increments of £5 - from 1st April 1914.
John H. Hocking, Inspector	Present salary maximum £125 to Sanitary increased to £140 per annum by 3 annual increments of £5 - from 1st July, 1914
E. Hadwin, Park-keeper	Present salary of 25/- per week (including house, fuel, light and rates) to be increased to 30/- per week by two annual increments of 2/6d. per week, the first of such increments to date from 1st April, 1914
R.D. Flanagan, Office Assistant, Engineer and Surveyor's Dept	Present 15/- per week to be increased to 17/6d. per week for the next financial year, further increasing to £55 per annum from 1st April, 1916, rising to £60 per annum for following financial year

BIBLIOGRAPHY

PRIMARY SOURCES

Birkenhead News 1901

Details of Deeds re West Kirby Park held at Birkenhead Central Library

Gore's Liverpool Directory 1901

Herald and Visitor Newspaper 1900-08

Hoylake and West Kirby Advertiser 1914-1915

Hoylake and West Kirby Board of Health Minutes 1891-1896

Hoylake and West Kirby Directory 1897

Hoylake UDC Finance Committee Minutes 1901-1905; 1907-1909

Hoylake UDC General Purposes and Parliamentary Committee Minutes 1896-1917

Hoylake and West Kirby Improvement Act 1900

Hoylake and West Kirby Local Board Minute Book 1893

Hoylake UDC Parks and Gardens and General Purposes Committee Minute Books 1896-1902; 1905-1915

Hoylake UDC Year Books 1900-1950

Kelly's Directory 1871

Moss's Directory of Hoylake and West Kirby 1906

Porter's Wirral Directory 1887

SECONDARY SOURCES

Brownbill, John *"West Kirby and Hilbre - A Parochial History"* Published by Henry Young & Sons Ltd., Liverpool, 1928

McInniss, Jean *"A Short History of Birkenhead Park"* Wirral Local Studies Group (undated)

Merseyside Railway History Society *"The Hooton to West Kirby Branch Line and the Wirral Way"* Published Metropolitan Borough of Wirral 1982

Millar, John *"Anything but Sailing"* Published John Millar (UK) Ltd., Hoylake, 1985

Mitchell, Alan *"The Trees of Britain and Northern Europe"* illustrated by John Wilkinson. Published Collins, London, 1982

Sanders, T W *"Encylopaedia of Gardening"* Published W.H. and L. Collingridge, London, 1910

The Community Programme for Wirral Borough Council Leisure Services Dept. *"Discovering Wirral's Parks - Ashton Park, West Kirby"*

INTERVIEWS

Mrs. Hilda (Dolly) Shipman nee Rutter (aged 99), gardener in Ashton Park during the First World War and Tennis Courts Attendant

Mrs. Lucy Smith nee Stanley (aged 95) whose father was Mr. J.J. Stanley, the first Park-keeper

REFERENCES

(1)   Hoylake and West Kirby Directory 1897

(2)   Parks and Gardens Committee Minutes, Hoylake UDC December 1900

(3)   Hoylake UDC Byelaws - January 1900

(4)   Hoylake and West Kirby Herald and Visitor January 1900

(5)   Birkenhead News - September 7th, 1901

(6)   Birkenhead News - September 14th 1901

(7)   Hoylake and West Kirby Herald and Visitor September, 1901

(8)   Parks and Gardens Committee - Hoylake UDC 1908

(9)   Parks and Gardens Committee - Hoylake UDC 1910

(10)   General Purposes and Parliamentary Committee Hoylake UDC - October, 1910

(11)   General Purposes and Parliamentary Committee Hoylake UDC - May, 1911